Novels for Students, Volume 26

Project Editor: Ira Mark Milne

Editorial: Jennifer Greve

Rights Acquisition and Management: Margaret Chamberlain-Gaston, Leitha Etheridge-Sims, Kelly Quin, Tracie Richardson Manufacturing: Drew Kalasky

Imaging and Multimedia: Lezlie Light Product Design: Pamela A. E. Galbreath, Jennifer Wahi Vendor Administration: Civie Green

Product Manager: Meggin Condino

For more information, contact
Gale
27500 Drake Rd.
Farmington Hills, MI 48331-3535

of the editors or publisher. Errors brought to the attention of the publisher and verified to the satisfaction of the publisher will be corrected in future editions.

ISBN-13: 978-0-7876-8683-3
ISBN-10: 0-7876-8683-2
eISBN-13: 978-1-4144-2933-5
eISBN-10: 1-4144-2933-9
ISSN 1094-3552

Printed in the United States of America
10 9 8 7 6 5 4 3 2 1

The Lord of the Rings

J. R. R. Tolkien 1954-1955

Introduction

The Lord of the Rings, by John Ronald Reuel Tolkien, first published in three parts during 1954 and 1955, is sometimes thought of as the first adult fantasy novel, although as a form it has affinity with the old heroic romances that inspired its author. Tolkien was a professor of Anglo-Saxon at Oxford and a scholar of such texts as *Beowulf*. His mythic quest novel, pitting a small hobbit as a hero against the Lord of Evil, holds a unique place in twentieth-century fiction: it is popular culture and enduring literature at the same time. It is a story about how goodness prevails, even in times of confusion and war, when people of integrity hold together. From the first, the book evoked strong, subjective reactions. In the fifty years following its publication, commentators learned to take an objective look at it.

Tolkien knew there was a hunger for heroic myth in the modern world, but he was surprised by his vast success. He would be even more overwhelmed at the games, toys, and films spawned by the novel, but he would understand the urge to proliferate what he had done. He hoped to sketch out a giant mythology that others could appreciate and add to, and they have. Not only has the fantasy industry grown up around the book, but also a demand for more details about his imaginary world, Middle-Earth. His son, Christopher, carried on, editing and publishing Tolkien's unfinished manuscripts. The amount of Middle-Earth history and chronicles published since the author's death is fourfold in volume to *The Hobbit* and *The Lord of the Rings* put together. Tolkien demonstrates that mythic stories speak to the human spirit in every age.

Author Biography

John Ronald Reuel Tolkien was born on January 3, 1892, in Bloemfontein, South Africa, of English parents, Mabel Suffield and Arthur Tolkien. His younger brother, Hilary, was born in 1894. In 1895, their mother took the children to England for a holiday, and while they were gone, their father died of rheumatic fever in South Africa. Mabel Tolkien was suddenly a widow in Birmingham, England, with two small children and very little income. She found a cottage in the country for the boys in Sarehole, Warwickshire, and the setting's effect on Ronald was deep. This was his ideal English countryside before industrialization, a hobbit landscape of villages and carts, an old brick mill, and lots of trees.

His mother was his first teacher, and from her, Ronald learned a love of languages and botany. He also loved fairy tales, adventure stories, and drawing. Meanwhile, she became a Catholic, to her family's dismay. This choice cut her off from their financial and emotional support, but Tolkien was proud of his mother's religious strength all his life. His strong Catholic faith came from her.

At the age of seven, he entered King Edward's School in Birmingham, and the family moved there. After two years, both boys were enrolled in a Catholic school, and the local priest, Father Francis Xavier Morgan, became the boys's guardian.

Because Ronald needed a more intellectual training, his mother enrolled him again at King Edward's on scholarship.

Mabel Tolkien died in 1904 of diabetes when Ronald was twelve. Though the orphans boarded with an aunt, Father Francis became their only real family. At King Edward's, Tolkien formed his first club, the TCBS (Tea Club and Barovian Society) with four close friends who all shared an interest in ancient languages and medieval studies. Tolkien even then was writing verse and inventing his first languages. The group dreamed of contributing something new to the world. This club helped him find a voice for his life work.

At the age of sixteen, Tolkien fell in love with nineteen-year-old Edith Bratt, another orphan in his boarding house. Father Francis forbade Tolkien to see or write to her until his twenty-first birthday, at which time they became engaged.

At Oxford, Tolkien studied comparative philology and ancient literature and went on inventing languages. When World War I broke out, he enlisted as a second lieutenant in a signaling corps, marrying Edith in 1916 before he left for France and the Battle of the Somme. In the trenches he began scribbling bits of his mythology, and when he returned to England to recuperate from trench fever, he continued his "Lost Tales," the germ of *The Silmarillion.*

After the war, Tolkien worked on staff at Oxford, then taught at Leeds University for three years, before settling as professor of Anglo Saxon at Oxford and raising his family of four children, John, Michael, Christopher, and Priscilla. His habit of inventing stories for the children led to *The Hobbit*, a children's story, published in 1937. In the same year, he began the sequel, *The Lord of the Rings*, which turned out to be for adults and wove in much of his mythology (published 1954-1955). *Farmer Giles of Ham* was published in 1949; "The Homecoming of Beortnoth Beorhthelm's Son," in 1953; *The Adventures of Tom Bombadil* in 1962; *Tree and Leaf* in 1964, and *Smith of Wootton Major* in 1967.

Media Adaptations

- Tolkien collaborated with composer Donald Swann in *The Road Goes Ever On: A Song Cycle*, the book and CD of poems from *The Lord of the Rings* set to music by Donald

Swann in 1967 and published by Harper Collins in 2003. Piano scores are beautifully illustrated with Tolkien's tengwar (elvish writing) and with comments on the elvish languages. Tolkien himself approved this arrangement. As of 2007, this production was available from Amazon.com and Amazon UK.

- *The Lord of the Rings* (Part One) was released in theaters as an animated film by Ralph Bakshi in 1978, produced by Saul Zaentz's Fantasy Films and distributed by United Artists. It includes the story up to Helm's Deep. The generally acknowledged critical failure of this version did not hurt its financial return. It led to Jackson's desire to do the live-action film. As of 2007, this version was available from Amazon.com.

- *The Return of the King* was released for television in 1980 as an animated film by Rankin-Bass to complete Bakshi's attempt. Warner Brothers released the Bakshi and Rankin-Bass versions along with Rankin-Bass's *The Hobbit* as a three-part series, *The Hobbit, The Lord of the Rings*, and *The Return of the King* on VHS and DVD. As of 2007, this version of *The Hobbit* was available on Amazon.com.

- *The Lord of the Rings* was read and sung by National Theatre and Royal Shakespeare Company actor Rob Inglis. It was produced in a CD format by HarperCollins in 1981, a complete production of fifty-one hours. As of 2007, Amazon.com made this version available.

- *The Lord of the Rings* appeared as a BBC Radio production. The abridged thirteen CDs included twenty-six half-hour shows dramatized by Brian Sibley with Ian Holm as narrator. As of 2007, this version could be ordered from Amazon.com.

- *Realms of Tolkien Images of Middle-Earth*, with illustrations by famous Tolkien artists, was produced by Harper Collins in 1996. Fifty-eight full-page color plates are included by artists such as Alan Lee, who influenced the look of *The Lord of the Rings* movies.

- *The Lord of the Rings*, the film trilogy on DVD (2002-2005), was produced by New Line Cinema. It includes: *The Fellowship of the Ring*, *The Two Towers*, and *The Return of the King*. Directed by

Peter Jackson and starring Ian McKellan, Elijah Wood, and Kate Blanchett, this elaborate adaptation shot in New Zealand won awards for special effects and art design. The in-depth DVD appendices with Tolkien experts and detailed explanations of how the film was made are as impressive as the film. As of 2007, this version was available from Amazon.com and in bookstores.

- One of many video games based on Tolkien's novel, *The Battle for Middle-Earth II* (2006) was produced by Electronic Arts. As of 2007, it was available in video game stores.

- *Map of Tolkien's Middle-Earth*, with text by Brian Sibley and illustrations by John Howe, is a fold-out with booklet published by HarperCollins in 2003. This version is very helpful in recreating the landscape of the stories and, as of 2007, was readily available in bookstores.

The American campus cult of Tolkien began in the 1960s, and Tolkien spent the last years of his life, too famous and busy to finish his great work of mythology. Edith died in 1971, and he died in 1973, at the age of eighty-one in Bournemouth, England. His son Christopher became his literary executor, publishing his unfinished work between 1975 and 1996.

Some of the awards Tolkien won are the International Fantasy Award for *The Lord of the Rings* in 1957; Fellowship in the Royal Society of Literature, 1957; Commander, Order of the British Empire, 1972; Gandalf Grand Master Award of the World Science Fiction Society for lifetime achievement, 1974; Gandalf Award for *The Silmarillion*, 1978; Locus Award for *The Silmarillion*, 1978; and the Mythopoeic Fantasy Award for *Unfinished Tales*, 1981.

The Fellowship of the Ring

BOOK ONE

The action takes place in Middle-Earth (Earth) at the end of the Third Age. The story opens in the Shire, the peaceful country of the hobbits, who are a small race, half the size of humans. At his eleventh-first birthday party, the hobbit Bilbo Baggins stages a spectacular departure from the Shire: he puts on a magic ring that he had found in his previous adventures (told about in *The Hobbit*) and disappears before the eyes of the guests. This is his joke, a way of escaping pesky relatives and a life that has become burdensome. He longs to travel again and return to Rivendell, home of the elves, and then settle down to write his memoirs.

He leaves his hobbit hole at Bag End, all his belongings, and the magic ring (at the wizard Gandalf's insistence) to his heir and nephew, Frodo Baggins. Some years later, Gandalf returns with alarming news: the magic ring is the One Ring of the Dark Lord, Sauron, who is trying to find it so he can control Middle-Earth. Sauron had fooled the elves into forging rings of power for every race; then he forged the One Ring to rule them all. The nine rings of men and seven of the dwarves are held by Sauron. Only the three elven rings are unsullied, used by the elves to preserve Middle-Earth. The

One evil Ring was cut off Sauron's finger in a war and lost till Bilbo got it from the creature Gollum on his adventures. Sauron knows the Ring is in the Shire, and so Frodo must leave with Sam, his servant, and if Gandalf does not show up to guide them (he does not), they must at least meet Gandalf later at the inn in Bree. Frodo is joined by his two friends, Merry and Pippin, and the four hobbits journey towards Bree by indirect ways, because they are being chased by Black Riders (the ghostlike Ringwraiths), servants of Sauron, who are always seeking the One Ring.

The hobbits take a detour through the Old Forest. There they meet Tom Bombadil who saves them from Old Man Willow and the barrow wights. When they finally get to Bree, Gandalf is still missing, and they do not know what to do. Gandalf has been delayed getting to Frodo because Saruman, the head of his order of wizards, has been corrupted by the Dark Lord. Saruman tempts Gandalf to join the dark side and, when he refuses, imprisons him. It takes some time for him to escape; Gandalf does not catch up with Frodo until Rivendell.

At the inn, Frodo accidentally slips on the Ring, becoming invisible. This immediately draws the Ringwraiths to him, for wearing the Ring puts the wearer into the world of shadow. The hobbits meet a strange man called Strider who says he is a Ranger from the north and friend of Gandalf. The Black Riders attack the inn, so they decide to trust Strider as a guide.

Strider takes them through the wilderness

towards Rivendell, an elf haven. The Black Riders catch them halfway at Weathertop, a ruined fort, and wound Frodo with a magic knife, causing him to hover between life and death. His companions rush him to Rivendell where Lord Elrond can save him. As they cross the Ford of Bruinen, Gandalf causes a flood that temporarily drowns the Black Riders.

BOOK TWO

watchtower

Frodo wakes up in Rivendell, healed by Elrond, though Gandalf says the wound will never heal completely. The hobbits rest, meet Bilbo and Gandalf again, and spend time singing and celebrating with the elves, lost in the wonder of their celestial land. Here Strider is revealed as Aragorn, the last heir of the Numenorean throne. He is a man betrothed to the elf maiden, Arwen, daughter of Elrond.

Elrond holds a council and invites representatives from all the free peoples of Middle-Earth. There it is decided that the only way to destroy Sauron and evil is to destroy the Ring itself. The Ring cannot be used, for it is a power that corrupts everyone around it. The hobbit Frodo is elected to be the Ringbearer and eight companions are chosen to go with him: three other hobbits, Gandalf the wizard, Aragorn the future king, Gimli the dwarf, Legolas the elf, and Boromir the warrior of Gondor. They are called the Fellowship of the Ring.

The Fellowship is blocked making its way over

the Caradhras mountain pass, so they turn and reluctantly go under the mountain through the mines of Moria, a dark place with many orcs or goblins. Gimli the dwarf finds the great underground city of Dwarrowdelf in ruins and his people extinct due to their greed in mining mithril, elf silver. The dwarves had awakened an ancient demon, a balrog, and the company also meet this balrog whom Gandalf fights, falling with it into the deeps of the Earth. The fellowship, grief-stricken, makes its way to Lothlórien, the greatest remaining elf kingdom. They are followed by the creature, Gollum, from whom Bilbo originally took the Ring and who miserably has been seeking it ever since. The Lady Galadriel, elven queen of great magic, gives presents and warns of treachery within the Fellowship.

Indeed, Boromir tries to take the ring from Frodo with the intention, he thinks, of using it to defend his city of Minas Tirith from the Dark Lord. The Ring has started corrupting the Company with a desire for power. Frodo puts on the Ring to escape Boromir and resolves to go on alone, but loyal Sam follows him. Meanwhile, Boromir is killed by orcs, and Merry and Pippin are captured and carried off. Aragorn, Gimli, and Legolas follow to rescue the remaining hobbits and leave Frodo and Sam to go to Mt. Doom.

The Two Towers

BOOK THREE

After Boromir's death, the Fellowship is split. Aragorn, Gimli, and Legolas chase the orcs who have captured Merry and Pippin. They leave Frodo to his own quest. Aragorn's party runs into the Riders of Rohan, the warriors of the plain, led by Eomer. Eomer's men have already destroyed the orcs in battle, and Merry and Pippin have escaped into Fangorn Forest. In Fangorn, the hobbits meet Treebeard, an ent, or walking tree, who herds and rules the forest. Treebeard laments that the evil wizard, Saruman, has cut down the trees of the forest for his war furnaces. Merry and Pippin rouse the ents to go to war, and they march towards Saruman's stronghold in Isengard.

When Aragorn's party enters Fangorn, they find not the hobbits, but the resurrected Gandalf, now Gandalf the White, who has been sent back from death to finish his task. He takes Aragorn and the others to the capital of Rohan to rouse the king, for war is about to break out on two fronts: one at Isengard, the fortress of the traitor, Saruman, and the other in Gondor with the army of the Dark Lord himself. Gandalf seeks to set up an alliance of free peoples to be ready.

Theoden, King of Rohan, is in bondage to Saruman who has put a spell on him. Gandalf breaks the spell, and once he has regained his strength, Theoden leads his warriors to the fortress of Helm's Deep with Eomer, Aragorn, Gimli, and Legolas to defend his people from Saruman's army. Just as Saruman's orcs are about to defeat Theoden, Gandalf appears at dawn with more men of Rohan, and the orcs of Isengard are defeated. Men chase the orcs underneath trees which have mysteriously appeared overnight on the plain. The orcs do not come out again. These are the walking trees of Fangorn Forest who play a part in the battle and who have destroyed the stronghold of Isengard.

Theoden, Gandalf, and the others march to Isengard and find Merry and Pippin with Treebeard, guarding Saruman and the ruins. Gandalf tries to get Saruman to come back to the allies, but Saruman refuses, so Gandalf breaks his magic staff. Pippin mischievously looks into a palantir, a seeing stone, revealing himself to the Dark Lord and confusing Sauron into thinking that Saruman has captured the hobbit with the Ring and that the Ring is thus at Isengard. This diverts his attention and buys the allies some time as Gandalf rides with Pippin to Gondor to rouse the Gondoreans. He leaves Aragorn at Rohan with Theoden's forces, ready to march for the Gondor front when he sends word.

BOOK FOUR

Sam and Frodo are lost on their way to Mordor to destroy the Ring. In the middle of the night, the creature Gollum is found near them, searching for the Ring. They ponder whether to kill him or bind him, but Frodo has pity on him, as Bilbo had. Gandalf had praised Bilbo's pity for sparing Gollum's life, saying that Gollum had some important part to play before the war was over. Now, Gollum becomes their guide into Mordor. Without Gollum's help, they could not have passed the Dead Marshes or found the Black Gate, entrance to Mordor. Frodo pities Gollum because he once bore the Ring, and now Frodo understands how the Ring destroys, for it is destroying him. It is becoming heavier and more evil the closer to the Dark Lord it gets. Frodo tries to save the schizophrenic Gollum, appealing to the hobbit nature he once bore, by calling him Smeagol, his former name when he was a hobbit like Frodo. Gollum tells them they cannot go through the Black Gate; they must go through a secret path that only he knows. Sam, however, remains skeptical of Gollum, naming his split personality, Slinker and Stinker.

While going through Ithilien, they meet Captain Faramir of Gondor, Boromir's brother, who is out on patrol with his men. Faramir finds out their secret mission but nobly does not stop them, because he learns how his brother fell from the evil influence of the Ring. The hobbits hear from Faramir that Gondor—the last Numenorean stronghold—is all that holds the Dark Lord from overrunning Middle-Earth. Faramir gives the hobbits provisions, and they continue on with Gollum to Cirith Ungol, a secret pass into Mordor.

The cave at the top of the pass is the lair of Shelob, the monstrous spider, which Gollum counts on to kill the hobbits so he can get the Ring. In the evil dark, Frodo pulls out the phial of Galadriel, containing starlight, which temporarily frightens Shelob away. But she bites Frodo, and Sam, thinking his master dead, wounds Shelob and escapes. He leaves behind the body of his master, taking up the Ring to continue the quest. When orcs come, he puts on the Ring to become invisible and, overhearing them speak, realizes that his master is not dead, only paralyzed. The orcs take Frodo, unconscious, to the tower of Cirith Ungol, and Sam cannot leave him but follows to see what he can do.

The Return of the King

BOOK FIVE

As Gandalf rides into the country of Gondor on his horse, Shadowfax, with Pippin, they see the beacons on the mountaintops lit, one after the other, as a signal that Gondor calls for aid in battle. They hurry to the capital city of Minas Tirith to speak to the Steward of Gondor, Denethor, the father of Boromir and Faramir. Minas Tirith is the city of the Numenorean kings of old, built on seven levels into the mountain. It is on the point of collapse, and Denethor is half mad from the loss of his son, Boromir, and from looking into a palantir to spy on the Dark Lord. He is suspicious of Gandalf and has heard rumors of Aragorn, the rightful heir to the throne. Gandalf urges him to prepare for war and counsels that Rohan will come to their aid.

Meanwhile, the remaining Rangers of the North and Elrond's sons come to Aragorn in Rohan, with the message that he must now fulfill his destiny and earn his kingship by taking the Paths of the Dead. Aragorn has looked into one of the palantirs and revealed himself to the Enemy, filling

Sauron with fear that the heir of the kings still lives with the sword that cut off the Ring from his finger, reforged now as Anduril, the Flame of the West. Aragorn hopes to provoke Sauron into a hasty attack, before his full strength forms.

Eowyn, sister of Eomer, falls in love with Aragorn, who gently refuses her because he is betrothed to the elf maiden, Arwen. Eowyn, in despair and in hope of military renown if she cannot have love, disguises herself as a warrior and secretly takes Merry with her to ride to Minas Tirith with the men of Rohan. Aragorn and his kin, as well as Gimli and Legolas, ride through the haunted mountains, the Paths of the Dead, to find their own way to Minas Tirith where the battle will be. An army of ghosts follows them. The ghosts are warriors who had broken their oaths to Aragorn's ancestor, and now, to find rest, they must follow him to fight for Gondor.

In Minas Tirith, Denethor sends Faramir on a hopeless mission to retake a post from the enemy. Faramir is wounded and thought to be dead by his father, who in his madness would burn them both alive in the tombs of their fathers. Pippin warns Gandalf, who saves Faramir, but Denethor dies.

The Siege of Gondor is in full swing, and the city ready to fall to Sauron's armies, though Gandalf commands what Gondorean troops there are. At dawn, they hear the horns of Rohan blowing; the horse lords have come to lift the siege. In the ensuing battle, the Chief Ringwraith on a winged beast attacks Theoden. Eowyn, disguised, defends her uncle and lord. The Ringwraith taunts her that no man may kill him. She reveals that she is a woman and kills his beastly steed. Together she and Merry finish the Chief Ringwraith as well. Theoden dies, and the allies are outnumbered, until suddenly, Aragorn and his ghost army show up to rout the enemy, for the time being.

Aragorn is allowed into Minas Tirith and accepted as the future king because he is able to heal the wounded, especially Faramir, Eowyn, and Merry. Then Gandalf comes up with a bold plan to attack Mordor directly, even though they are outnumbered, to divert the attention of Sauron and give Frodo more time to complete his mission. All the army of the West moves south to the Black Gate and fights an orc army that will surely win.

BOOK SIX

Frodo awakens in the tower of Cirith Ungol, thinking the enemy has taken the Ring. Sam, tricking the orcs into killing each other, climbs the tower and sets Frodo free, returning the Ring to him. They set off towards Mt. Doom. Frodo and Sam struggle on through the desolate land of Mordor with little food and water, and little hope. Sam has to assume leadership, as Frodo is weak and delirious from carrying the Ring. The Eye of Sauron is diverted to Aragorn's army at the Black Gate.

Sam carries Frodo on his back the last part of the journey up Mt. Doom. Suddenly, Gollum reappears and fights Frodo for the Ring. Sam guards Gollum while Frodo goes to the brink of the volcano to throw in the Ring. At the last moment, Frodo cannot destroy the Ring. Gollum escapes Sam and attacks Frodo who puts on the Ring to become invisible, but Gollum will not let go and bites the Ring off Frodo's finger. Gollum, triumphant, dances for a moment with the Ring on the brink, then trips and falls into the fiery chasm with it. The mountain erupts, and Sam leads Frodo out to a spot on the mountain to await death together, their mission accomplished.

Meanwhile, at the Black Gate, the Captains of the West are foundering until the giant eagles come to aid them. In the middle of this chaos, an earthquake topples the towers of the Black Gate and darkness covers the land. Gandalf knows this means that Frodo's mission has been successful, and the reign of Sauron has ended. Gandalf calls down one of the giant eagles and rides on its back to Mt. Doom, rescuing Sam and Frodo from the erupting volcano.

Aragorn is crowned king, and the Fourth Age of Men begins. Faramir weds Eowyn, and Aragorn weds Arwen, who must give up her elven immortality to live a mortal life. Her place on the last elven ship to leave Middle-Earth is given to Frodo whose wound will never heal. After the hobbits return to the Shire as heroes, they rid the Shire of the evil men who had crept in during Sauron's time, and Sam becomes the new mayor. When Frodo finishes his memoirs, he takes the last elven ship with Gandalf, Galadriel, Elrond, and all the elves to the Blessed Lands of the West.

Appendices

Appendices cover material from the mythology which Tolkien could not fit into the novel. Appendix A tells the history of Numenorean Kings, the history of Gondor, and the tale of Aragorn and Arwen. Appendix B is a chronology of the Ages of Middle-Earth. Appendix C contains family trees of the hobbits. Appendix D describes the Calendars of Middle-Earth. Appendix E explains the pronunciation and alphabets of Tolkien's invented languages for Middle-Earth. Appendix F is a fuller explanation of the languages of various races of Middle-Earth: elves, men, hobbits, orcs, ents, and dwarves.

Characters

Aragorn

Also called Strider, Dunedan, Elessar, and
Estel, Aragorn, son of Arathorn, is a long lived
Numenorean man, heir of Isildur and the throne of
Gondor. He is raised by Elrond in Rivendell, where
he falls in love with Elrond's daughter, Arwen. He
wanders Middle-Earth in disguise as a Ranger,
helping Gandalf keep track of the doings of the
Enemy. He is suspected by the hobbits at first
because of his rough appearance, but once they get
to Rivendell where Strider the Ranger is known as
Aragorn, the heir of Isildur, they form a different
opinion, because he takes on his true, noble
appearance. He guides the hobbits from Bree to
Rivendell and becomes one of the Fellowship. He is
later crowned King of Gondor by Gandalf. A wise,
resourceful, and humble man, worthy of being king,
he is called Estel by the elves, meaning hope.
Elessar refers to the green Elfstone jewel presented
to him by Galadriel. Dunedan means one of the
Northern Rangers, last of the Numenorean men in
the north.

Bilbo Baggins

Bilbo is a hobbit of the Shire who first finds
the Ring and takes it from Gollum in the tunnels of
the Misty Mountains (as explained in *The Hobbit*).

Hobbits are Halflings, three to four feet tall, peaceful, and fond of food and drink and a good pipe. They have hairy feet and go barefoot. Bilbo is a fun-loving and clever trickster, good at riddle lore. His greatest act is his pity in sparing the life of Gollum, who becomes important in the quest to destroy the Ring. The Ring abnormally prolongs Bilbo's life. He gives it reluctantly to Frodo and retires to the elves in Rivendell where he writes songs and his memoirs. Bilbo was fortunate in being relatively untouched by the Ring's evil. His elven sword, Sting, whose blade turns blue when orcs are near, and his precious chain mail of mithril, are given to Frodo.

Frodo Baggins

Frodo is Bilbo's nephew and heir. Frodo is more aristocratic and noble than the other hobbits. He is well read in the lore of Middle-Earth and speaks Elvish. He becomes the main hero, whose task is to destroy the Ring of evil so Sauron will not control Middle-Earth. He is wounded by a Ringwraith, and the wound never completely heals. The evil Ring nearly drives him mad, and he is unable to throw it into Mt. Doom at the last minute. He is followed throughout his adventure by his faithful servant, Samwise Gamgee, and by the creature Gollum, both character doubles for Frodo, showing his good and bad potential. Like the wounded King Arthur, Frodo does not exactly die but is allowed to leave in the last ship of the elves for the Blessed Lands as a reward for his great sacrifice to Middle-Earth.

Tom Bombadil

Tom is a nature spirit of the Old Forest who looks clownish in his bright blue jacket and yellow boots. He speaks in rhyme, saving the hobbits from Old Man Willow and the barrow wights. He and Goldberry, his lady, entertain the hobbits and help them get to Bree. Tom is called a "master" of the forest, one of the oldest beings of Middle-Earth, and the only character not interested in the Ring or Sauron.

Boromir

Boromir, son of Denethor, is son of the ruling Steward of Gondor. Boromir is a hearty warrior, good but rash, a man of action. Though chosen as one of the Fellowship to help Frodo, he is overcome by lust for the Ring that he thinks will help defend his beloved city of Minas Tirith. He wants to give it as a mighty gift for his father to use in fighting Sauron. After he scares Frodo away, he is killed by orcs, trying to protect the other hobbits. He carries a horn that he blows at time of need.

Meriadoc Brandybuck

Meriadoc, or Merry, is a hobbit of the Shire. He is a Bucklander, one of the more independent hobbits, considered a bit outlandish because Bucklanders boat on the river and go into the Old

Forest. Merry has maturity and more lore of the world than most hobbits. He is paired with Pippin, his cousin and friend, and considered the older and steadier of the two. He becomes squire to King Theoden and a hero on the battlefield of Pelennor Fields when he kills the chief Ringwraith.

Denethor

Denethor is Steward of Gondor, who holds the throne until the return of a king. Denethor is from the failing line of Numenorean men, ruling over the capital city, Minas Tirith, about to be destroyed by Sauron. He is a proud and stubborn man, a tragic hero, who means well but lacks sound judgment. In his desperation he has looked into a palantir, or seeing stone, and spied on the Enemy. This has made him mad. He irrationally favors his son, Boromir, over his son, Faramir and sends Faramir on a suicide mission. He kills himself out of despair, believing all is lost with Boromir dead and Faramir wounded. He sets himself on fire, as though already dead himself, leaving the city to fend for itself in its darkest hour.

Elrond

Elrond is Halfelven, the son of an elf and human. He is Lord of Rivendell or Imladris, an elven stronghold protected by magic. Aragorn was hidden and raised here by Elrond for protection as the last surviving heir to Gondor's throne. Many of the precious treasures of Middle-Earth, such as the shards of Narsil, the sword that cut off the Ring from Sauron's finger, are preserved at Rivendell. Elrond bears one of the three great rings, Vilya, the blue stone of air. The rings preserve and protect Middle-Earth. Elrond has chosen immortality, as his daughter, Arwen, chooses mortality when she marries Aragorn. Elrond is one of the wisest leaders, a friend of Gandalf, committed to preserving Middle-Earth from the Dark Lord, whom he fought in the previous age. He hosts the Council of all free peoples to decide the fate of the Ring.

Eomer

Eomer is nephew and heir of King Theoden of Rohan, who is banished with his men when Theoden falls under the spell of the evil counselor, Wormtongue. Eomer is loyal to the king and is recalled when Gandalf cures Theoden. Eomer is a brave warrior and fights at Theoden's side at Helm's Deep and on the Pelennor Fields. He becomes friends with Aragorn, and when his uncle dies in battle, he succeeds him as King of Rohan. The ethic of the Rohirrim is exhibited by Eomer on the battlefield when he sings and laughs in the face of despair.

Eowyn

Lady Eowyn is the beautiful and slender sister of Eomer and niece of King Theoden, who treats her as a daughter. Eowyn and Eomer are close as brother and sister, but he councils her always against fighting in the war. She is a proud shield-maiden, trained to fight, and fears being stranded in a woman's inactive life. She falls in adolescent love with Aragorn, who gently refuses her. Though Theoden leaves her to rule the people while he goes to battle, she disguises herself as the warrior Dernhelm and rides with Merry into war. She is wounded defending her uncle from the Chief Ringwraith and cured of her wounds by Aragorn; afterwards, she marries Faramir.

Faramir

Faramir, younger son of Denethor, is a Ranger of Ithilien, guarding Gondor from the spies of Mordor on the border. He is wiser than his brother, Boromir, more like Aragorn or Gandalf in nature. He captures Sam and Frodo on their way to Mordor but nobly lets them go and helps them towards their goal, thus succeeding where his brother failed, as he does not take the Ring. After the wars, Aragorn makes Faramir the Steward of Gondor, and he weds Eowyn, thus cementing the alliance between Gondor and Rohan.

Galadriel

Galadriel, elven queen of Lothlórien with the golden hair, is the most powerful elf left in Middle-Earth. She is tall, beautiful, and wise. She sees past, present, and future in her mirror. She bears one of the three rings of power, Nenya, the ring of adamant, ruling water. The Lady of the Wood presents important gifts to the Fellowship for their success. Galadriel was one of the ancient elves who came to Middle-Earth to protect and teach men, but she refused to obey the gods when the elves were ordered to go back to Valinor, land of the gods. Because she helped defeat Sauron and refused the temptation of the Ring when Frodo offered it to her, she was allowed to go finally to the Blessed Lands on the last ship with her consort, Celeborn, and Gandalf, Elrond, Bilbo, and Frodo.

Samwise Gamgee

Samwise is a hobbit of the Shire, servant of Frodo, and his companion on the quest. Sam is Frodo's humble gardener; his devotion to his master is so absolute that he never thinks of himself or of stealing the Ring. He has a lower class dialect and sense of humor; he is cheerful, a good cook and storyteller, and he composes songs and loves to be with the elves. Sam is in only one way less admirable than Frodo. He sees the worst in Gollum and does not have Frodo's pity or understanding for the ruined creature, thus provoking Gollum's worst side at the wrong time. Without Sam, Frodo could not have completed his journey. Tolkien thought Sam more interesting in character than Frodo, who had to be more noble and rarefied as the main hero.

Gandalf

Gandalf, called Mithrandir or Grey Pilgrim by the elves, is one of the five wizards who are Maiar (angelic beings) sent to protect Middle-Earth. Gandalf has the appearance of an old man; he begins as the humble Gandalf the Grey, clothed in a grey robe and pointed hat, traveling from one land to another, like Aragorn, his friend, keeping an eye on things in the quiet before the Dark Lord begins his war. He wears one of the three rings of power, Narya the red fire, the kindler that helps him rouse all the peoples to join together. Gandalf is the wisest teacher, the kingmaker, like Merlin to Arthur. He is betrayed and imprisoned by Saruman the White, the head of his order, who has been corrupted by looking into a palantir. Gandalf falls to his death fighting the Balrog in Moria but, being one of the immortals, is resurrected and comes back to finish his task as Gandalf the White, replacing Saruman. He rides Shadowfax, the fastest horse in Middle-Earth; bears the elven sword, Glamdring; and carries a magic staff that creates light in dark places. He is a little stern and inscrutable in manner, but kind at heart. He is not allowed by the higher powers to interfere with Middle-Earth matters directly but seeks to defeat evil by inspiring and teaching those around him. When his task is done, he leaves Middle-Earth on the last elven ship for the Blessed Isles.

Gimli

Gimli is the son of Gloin, one of the dwarves from Bilbo's adventures. He is part of the Fellowship that sets out from Rivendell, representing the dwarf folk. Gimli carries an axe and is a fierce fighter. He is stubborn and irascible, but makes friends with Legolas, though dwarves and elves usually detest each other. His cousin, Balin, is Lord of Moria, the underground dwarf kingdom the company passes through. Gimli is loyal to Aragorn, following him even to the Paths of the Dead. He also becomes passionately devoted to Galadriel after passing through Lorien, obtaining the gift of three gold hairs from her head.

Gollum

Gollum, the slimy and twisted creature, was once a hobbit called Smeagol. He killed his friend Deagol, who found the Ring in the river. Gollum choked his friend and ever after makes an involuntary swallowing noise, "gollum." Gollum uses his invisibility to steal things, but eventually he is outcast from his kind, hating the light of day and hiding away in caves. The Ring prolongs his miserable life, until it falls in the cave, and Bilbo picks it up. Gollum, like the Ringwraiths, searches ever after for the Ring, secretly following Frodo and Company. Frodo lets Gollum be his guide to Mordor against Sam's judgment. Sam names Gollum's split personality "Slinker" and "Stinker," the whining victim and the malicious aggressor. Nevertheless, it is Gollum who finishes the quest by falling into Mt. Doom with the Ring. It was this prediction of Gandalf's, that Gollum had some part to play, that stayed Frodo's hand from killing him earlier.

Legolas

Legolas is a woodland elf, one of the Fellowship, son of Thranduil, king of the Mirkwood elves. Legolas has attributes of his kindred—he can see farther than humans, is intuitive, and walks lightly above the ground. He is agile and a good fighter, using bow and arrows. Elves are immortal but can be killed in battle. He becomes best friends with a dwarf, Gimli, which is unheard of, for the two races typically detest each other. Legolas sings the glories of trees and forests; Gimli of mining in caves. They stick by each other in battle.

Merry

See Meriadoc Brandybuck

Pippin

See Peregrin Took

Saruman

Saruman is the White Wizard, the head of the Order of Wizards, who becomes corrupt. Saruman lives in Isengard in the tower of Orthanc, studying the lore of Middle-Earth. He is seduced to the side of the Dark Lordwhen he looks into a palantir. He does not understand that he is a tool of Sauron. He turns Orthanc into a war factory, making explosives and breeding orcs or warrior demons (called Uruk-hai) that are more terrible than the Dark Lord's. His orcs bear a white hand on their armor. Saruman's main weapon is his voice, which can bend others to his will. He attempts to seduce Gandalf to the dark side, saying they will be partners with Sauron. He stirs up war, sending out his armies against Rohan. He is defeated at Helm's Deep. Gandalf breaks Saruman's staff, but he slinks off to do what evil he can in the Shire as Sharkey. Eventually, he is killed by his own minion, Wormtongue.

Sauron

Sauron, the Dark Lord of Mordor, is the evil Enemy of Middle-Earth. He was once a Maia (angel) and lieutenant of Melkor, the Valar (god) who fell. When Melkor was destroyed, Sauron arose to take his place. He fooled the elves into creating the rings of power, and then he created the One Ring to rule them all. He controls the nine rings of men, the seven of the dwarves, but the three elven rings are hidden from him. In the Third Age, Sauron has no visible shape but dwells in Mordor, building a great army in the wasteland around Mt. Doom. All his power has been poured into the One Ring, which was cut off his finger by Isildur, Aragorn's ancestor, in the Second Age. Sauron appears in the palantir only as a fiery eye that does not sleep but can see everything in Middle-Earth. He is served by the Nazgul, or Ringwraiths, the ghosts of the kings of men, and by orcs, the demons who are corrupted elves. He is immortal, so when he is destroyed in one form, he takes another when he regains strength. The Third Age and Sauron's power are destroyed when the Ring is destroyed.

Topics for Further Study

- Research the stages of the quest in Part I of Joseph Campbell's *The Hero with a Thousand Faces*. Write a paper applying those stages to Frodo's quest in *The Lord of the Rings*. Does Frodo fit the average quest pattern? How does he make the Atonement with the Father? How does he cross the return threshold? If you can make a case for Sam going farther than Frodo on the quest by accomplishing the step called The Master of Two Worlds, then do so.

- Discuss with your classmates what makes Aragorn fit to be king. Is it because he is Aragorn, son of

Arathorn, the wielder of the heirloom sword, Anduril, or is it his leadership ability? Name Aragorn's abilities as a leader. List the qualities, such as courage, and then find examples in the book that substantiate that quality. Based on hints from the book, imagine how his reign will change Middle-Earth. How will he solve problems? Do research to find an historical king who had similar qualities or circumstances and write a report on kingship in history and in fantasy.

- Research the role of women in Anglo-Saxon society and comment on Eowyn's desire to go to war. Were women trained to fight with weapons? Were men and women equal in that society? Give a report on your findings or write a poem or short story on Eowyn's Dream of Glory. Imagine she is a young girl on the threshold of life, dreaming of her future.

- Summarize the differences between book and film versions of *The Lord of the Rings.* Watch the DVD commentaries of the Jackson film and give a report on how the writers adapted the story for film. Did Jackson do a good job as director?

What would you have done differently if you were making the film? Which version, book or film, do you like better and why? Comment in general on what one must do to adapt a novel to film.

- Compare the elves in Tolkien's story to other stories of fairies and elves. How are Tolkien's elves distinctive? Why do they leave Middle-Earth at the end of the Third Age? Find drawings of elves and fairies to illustrate your points. Create a fairy scrapbook with comments interspersed with illustrations. Do this as a group project, then present it to the rest of the class.

- How was World War I, the war in which Tolkien participated, similar to and different from the War of the Ring? Were battle conditions and movements the same? Were the codes of war the same or different? Which were the best warriors in Middle-Earth and why? Does Tolkien paint war realistically or unrealistically? What does the novel show readers about the effectiveness of war as a solution? Create a research journal with the answers, giving examples from the novel and history.

Theoden

Theoden is King of Rohan, land of the horse lords or Rohirrim. His hall, Meduseld, is something like a Viking hall with its armed warriors. Rohirrim are men (speaking Anglo-Saxon and living in that kind of culture), not as noble or long lived as the Numenoreans, but with a long and honorable warrior tradition. Theoden is bewitched into senility by Saruman, letting Wormtongue, Saruman's lackey, make his decisions for him. When Gandalf breaks the spell on him, he takes action as the noble chieftain he is, a model to his men, calling on the Rohirrim to rally. Aragorn fights at his side at Helm's Deep, and in turn, Theoden goes to the aid of Gondor, where he falls on Pelennor Fields in full honor. His niece, Eowyn, is wounded trying to save him, and his nephew, Eomer, succeeds him as king.

Peregrin Took

Peregrin Took or Pippin, hobbit of the Shire, cousin of Merry (Meriadoc Brandybuck) is the comic relief. The Tooks are considered adventurous for hobbits. Lighthearted and mischievous, Pippin causes trouble to the Fellowship by being curious at the wrong times: he rouses the Balrog in Moria and looks in the forbidden palantir. Pippin becomes squire to Denethor and helps save Faramir's life in Minas Tirith when Denethor tries to burn him on his own funeral pyre.

Treebeard

Treebeard is an ent, or treeherder. An ent is a tree that can walk, taking care of the other trees who are not awake. The ents are sad because they have lost their entwives, who left them eons ago, preferring gardens to forests, and there are no more entings, or descendents. Treebeard speaks slowly because ents are long lived and think slowly. He is a friend of Gandalf but becomes an enemy of Saruman, who is destroying the trees. Pippin and Merry convince the ents to go to war. The ents destroy orcs and dismantle the stones of Isengard, Saruman's stronghold.

Arwen Undomiel

Arwen, called the Evenstar of her people, is an immortal dark-haired elf-maiden, daughter of Elrond. She foregoes her immortality to marry Aragorn and ennoble his line of kings in the Fourth Age. Elrond has forbidden their marriage until Aragorn overcomes the Enemy and takes the throne. She is Galadriel's granddaughter and makes a banner for Aragorn to carry into battle.

Providence

    The Lord of the Rings demonstrates the theme of Providence, the medieval doctrine that holds that God works out everything to a right end. The righteous prevail. The attacks of the Dark Lord ultimately unite the free peoples of Middle-Earth and bring back a golden age with the rightful king. Gollum, a nasty character who tries to defeat the quest, is the one who actually destroys the Ring and achieves the quest. Gandalf falls to his death, only to arise as the more powerful Gandalf the White. Tolkien does not name God directly, but the work suggests that a divine justice rules Middle-Earth. Gandalf tells Frodo that the Dark Lord does not know everything: "Behind [Bilbo's finding the Ring] there was something else at work, beyond any design of the Ring-maker.... Bilbo was *meant* to find the Ring, and *not* by its maker." Gandalf convinces Frodo he is also meant to have it, and since it is a divine mission given to Frodo, he must be worthy and capable of taking on the quest.

Power Corrupts

    The One Ring is the Ring of Power, and it destroys everyone who tries to possess it. Thus, Tolkien implies that since the Ring embodies the Dark Lord, it is the desire for power over others that corrupts. Frodo unconsciously tests each main character for strength of integrity. He offers the Ring to Tom Bombadil, Gandalf, Aragorn, Elrond, and Galadriel. They all refuse, showing they are just. Boromir fails the test by trying to get the Ring from Frodo, but his brother Faramir passes by refusing it. The desire for the Ring destroys Gollum, Saruman, and Denethor. Sam is able to carry it without harm because of his devotion to his master. Frodo is strong until the last minute when he is unable to part with the Ring on his own. The Ring of Power is shown to be untrustworthy and deceiving, a symbol of lust for domination that must be actively refused by every good soul.

The Haunting Sense of History

The sense of history alive in the present, an elegiac feel of a more glorious past slipping away, is present in every culture of Middle-Earth through songs and legends. It is the end of the Third Age, and readers are reminded of the fading power of the elves, who are leaving Middle-Earth; the lost kingdom of Numenor, sunk like Atlantis, and the continued failure of that line of men in Gondor; the fewer numbers and strength of the Rohirrim; the fall of Khazad-dum, the great Dwarf city; and the growing threat to the Shire, that had always been safe. Faramir calls Gondor "Men of the Twilight." None of the races is able to keep their precious heritage intact, with the threat of war ever present.

Friendship as the Basis of Strength

Friendship is not to be underestimated, for though the Allies are fewer than the armies of the Dark Lord, they are bound in love and loyalty, a unity that counts for more than numbers. Individual initiative is not prized, as in modern action films. Teamwork and loyalty are the key virtues. Friendship is evident in the bond between the hobbits, especially Frodo and Sam, who only make it up Mt. Doom together; and in the Fellowship of the different races of Middle-Earth, who accompany and support the Ringbearer. It is the alliance of good people and of friends that overcomes the Enemy. It takes everyone working together, everyone a hero, to outsmart and defeat evil. Community is a corollary of the friendship theme— what binds the different lands together in internal harmony and tradition, such as the Shire, Rivendell, and Rohan. Each land is shown to enrich the fabric of the whole of Middle-Earth. Diversity and interdependence are values that Gandalf stands for, as he rides through the countryside, rousing each group to support the other.

Courage Against the Odds

Courage against overwhelming odds is a theme Tolkien lifted from Norse sagas. He loved heroes like Beowulf, whose honor and fame lived on, even though he faced unbeatable foes and died to save his people. The brave heart that endures is noble in victory or defeat. Heroism does not depend on size or gender (e.g., the hobbits are Halflings, and Eowyn is a woman) or outcome (Theoden dies honorably in battle). Frodo is constantly worried that he will not have enough courage to carry out what he knows must be done, but he finds it within himself at each crisis. Tolkien's heroes have to face their fears, not just walk through their parts.

War Does Not Defeat Evil

Though Gandalf urges an assault on the Black Gate, he explains that evil is not defeated through war: "I still hope for victory, but not by arms." War is a necessary evil, a self-defense, but it does not stop Sauron. As Faramir explains to Frodo, warfare is not the ultimate solution; it destroys both sides. Frodo's quest to destroy the One Ring of Power is ultimately an internal moral battle and is fought on that high ground: the message is that people must be willing to sacrifice domination for the good of all.

Heroism Depends on Free Will

Although Providence rules Middle-Earth, each character must choose the good out of free will. Frodo was meant to have the Ring and go on the quest, but he did not have to accept the burden. At each stage of the quest, he has to choose whether to go on. At Amon Hen, Frodo contends with the Eye of Sauron and Gandalf's voice, each urging him on a different course. These are in his mind, symbolizing the power of good and evil in each person. "Suddenly he was aware of himself again. Frodo,

neither the Voice nor the Eye: free to choose."
Frodo chooses the good for himself.

Evil Defeats Itself

The Dark Lord loses because he is not as imaginative as the good characters who have a larger viewpoint—the good of the whole. The Dark Lord does not imagine the allies would seek to destroy the Ring; he imagines they want power, as he does. The demonic orcs always outnumber the allies, but they are quarrelsome, envious, hateful, ambitious, and suspicious. Evil is often shown to be a corruption of the good, insubstantial in itself. For instance, Sauron himself was once, like Satan, an angelic being of light. The orcs were once elves. Gollum was once a hobbit. Tolkien seems to have it both ways, making evil an external and internal force, an active malice and a mere distortion of good. Boromir, for example, is a good man who falls because of the outer temptation of the Ring, but he is attracted to it from his own inner weakness as well.

The Spoiling of Nature Is Demonic

Tolkien dearly loved the world of unspoiled nature, especially trees. He hated the industrialization of the modern world that was destroying nature. Saruman's war factory at Orthanc demands the stripping of trees from Fangorn Forest, and the revenge of the trees, under Treebeard, is perhaps his desire to see balance in nature restored.

The Land of Mordor is a barren land of ash and waste, not unlike a land destroyed by war or industrialization.

The Desire to Create Is Divine

The creative urge in humans, who according to Tolkien's belief are made in the image of God, is explored in the race of elves, who are actually glorified humans. Their desire to make Middle-Earth beautiful and abundant is seen in their civilizations among trees and river valleys that preserve all that is good and beautiful. Tolkien sees the making of fantasy itself as an elven craft, a vision of how things are and could be.

Fantasy Novel

Fantasy is a type of story that takes place in a non-existent world, often used to comment on the contemporary world, as is the case with this novel. Tolkien has been credited with the invention of modern fantasy, though of course, the fantastic itself is an ancient mode of storytelling (seen for example in *The Arabian Nights* and the *Odyssey*). Though some critics deny that modern fantasy is literature, Tolkien saw the genre as belonging to that category of literature which has to do with a spiritual journey and serious purpose. He defined this type of literature in his essay "On Fairy Stories." The fantasist engages in what he called subcreation, making an alternative world, in order to help readers see in enriched form what is already in this world. The story provides consolation through a eucatastrophe (happy ending), and that is important because it mimics grace and denies a final victory by evil.

Heroic Romance

Tolkien himself did not call *The Lord of the Rings* fantasy; he called it mythic or heroic romance. A myth is a story of creation and the gods. Tolkien's complete mythology of Middle-Earth, told in *The Silmarillion* and the appendices of the novel, is felt in the background of the novel's action, giving it its large scope. Readers are aware that the story takes place in the Third Age, that two more glorious ages have preceded and one lesser one follows without magic in it. These are the imagined early cycles of the Earth, the ages of heroes. Heroic or epic stories concern the legendary heroes of any culture. The romance, or long tale with supernatural elements such as demons and magicians, is the form of the tale often chosen for telling about heroes (such as *Beowulf* in Anglo-Saxon literature). The epic tale (e.g., *Odyssey*) concerns heroes who save or renew a civilization in crisis, and it has certain conventions that Tolkien uses freely; for instance, the ornate weapons and architecture and customs of each place exhibiting the nature of the character or country. The hobbits are armed from the weaponry in the mounds of the Numenoreans, which is a reference to a superior, lost culture behind their own small Shire. Heroic characters, such as Theoden, Boromir, Legolas, Gimli, and Eomer, are more types than realistic portraits. They frequently engage in long conversations that are set pieces, such as at the Council of Elrond. The book is also constructed around Tolkien's invented languages (fourteen in all), which are peppered throughout as names, place names, songs, poems, and legends. Names and words are thus not so much symbols, as direct invocations of lost races or heroes, evident in the song of Earendil, for instance, in which the hero becomes a star, whose light Frodo holds in physical form in the phial of Galadriel, to guide him. As a linguist, Tolkien knew the rules of languages and could make whole cultures out of the roots of his invented words. His genius in naming places and characters conveys the sense that they exist. Tolkien gives the book the weight and feel of history. The story appeals to many modern readers because it has blended elements of many genres; it is finally a novel because the events are treated at length as everyday reality. Tolkien carefully coordinates all details, like the phases of the moon and the dates.

Compare & Contrast

- **1950s:** The cold war persists between the United States and the Soviet Union. The novel reminds readers of World War II, which ends in 1945. Readers see parallels between Sauron and Hitler and between Rohan, Gondor, the Shire, and the Western Allies, Britain, the United States, and France.

  Today: Readers see a parallel between the novel and President Bush's war on terrorism, with Bush as either Aragorn saving Middle-Earth or as Sauron trying to dominate Iraq. About.com. posts a doctored photo of Bush with the Ring of Power on his finger sitting at his desk in the Oval office (politicalhumor.about.com).

- **1950s:** Edmund Wilson and other

critics attack Tolkien for his handling of female characters, saying there are almost none, and the few portrayed are stereotyped.

Today: The Girl-Power effect increases in Hollywood in the 2000s after the example of the movie *Alien* with an independent female lead. Fantasy heroines, such as Xena, Buffy, Wonder Woman, and Princess Leia, are popular draws in film and video games.

- **1950s:** Deforestation is still accepted as a necessary price for urban progress in Great Britain and elsewhere in the world, with only a relatively small number of vocal opponents.

  Today: The total woodland of Great Britain is 2.5 percent of its land area, with 45 percent of the ancient and semi-natural woodland that existed after World War II lost since that time. The government of the U.K. has a policy to increase woodland planting by 5,000 hectares a year.

The Quest Journey

The Lord of the Rings is structured as a quest

journey. The omniscient third person narrator tells the story, basically around the journey of Frodo's quest through the fantastic world of Middle-Earth (Earth in its imagined ancient history) to Mount Doom and back again, but there are digressions; for instance, through the Old Forest where they meet Tom Bombadil. The digressions do not detract from the tightly woven and unified plot. The narrator is perfectly aware of the importance of the events ending the Third Age, and so each episode, whether told chronologically or picked up out of sequence, is handled with suspense that moves the plot in the direction of the climax of the Ring's destruction. The narrator's formal and archaic sounding English, heroic and prophetic in tone, helps provide authority to his vision, almost giving the feel of scripture.

The publisher insisted it was too expensive to make one novel of a million words and a thousand pages, so the three separate novels were created, based on Tolkien's divisions of the work into six books. Each title covers two books. The first two books have a linear structure—the forward journey of Frodo and the Fellowship. "The Two Towers" begins the more intricate interlaced structure in which Tolkien hops from one group of characters to another, after the Fellowship breaks up. Some have seen this design as a flaw, contrary to modern novels that intercut more closely between stories, as happens in film. Possibly Tolkien was influenced by medieval literature in his design. In any case, the interlace works to build suspense: he follows Aragorn and Gandalf for a while, then backtracks to pick up Frodo and Sam. The starting and ending point of the journey is the Shire, the home of the hobbits. Like the usual mythic journey, the starting point is a version of everyday reality, the mundane hobbit life in the foreground. By the time the hobbits reach the Old Forest, however, they have crossed the boundary into a magic world where trees can sing and Tom, the nature spirit, is there to save them.

Tolkien, the Philologist

Tolkien's thinking was historical; a professor of Anglo-Saxon, Tolkien was immersed in the study of languages and old sagas. Using his knowledge of linguistic laws, he created his own languages with logical morphological changes. The Elven tongue Quenya was inspired by the Finnish language in *The Kalevala*, and the Elven tongue, Sindarin, was similar to Welsh. These imagined languages are the basis of his Middle-Earth mythology, for he said he had to invent people to speak his languages. The languages are so complex that linguists still study them, and people try to learn them. From the invented languages and the meanings of the roots of those words, he reconstructed missing parts of the Earth's history, as it might have been, with all the various races of beings: hobbits, dwarves, elves, men, ents, gods, orcs, demons, dragons. The novel is an epic, set as Tolkien saw it, in the imagined pre-history of the present Earth (called Middle-Earth after the name of the Earth in *Beowulf*).

The Four Ages of Middle-Earth

Tolkien follows the scheme of four cosmological ages as in Greek mythology, with the First Age of Middle-Earth, a golden age (retold in *The Silmarillion*); the Second Age, a silver age, declining in value but still glorious with the civilization of Numenor (Atlantis). The sinking of Numenor, and the Last Alliance of Men and Elves when the One Ring was cut from Sauron's hand ends the Second Age. The Third Age, the time of the novel, is a nostalgic time in which beings look back to earlier glory. The elves are still on Earth, preserving it with their rings of power, but Sauron, the Dark Lord, is looking for his lost Ring and threatening once more to destroy Middle-Earth. The wizard Gandalf is a Maia, or angelic being, sent to Earth to help rouse the races to defeat Sauron. With Sauron's defeat, the elves leave, and the Fourth Age of the rule of men begins with Aragorn's reign. Though the Fourth Age starts with a golden time ruled by the true king, it is implied that this will be an Earth more like the present one, without magic.

World War II

The novel was begun in 1937 and was written largely during World War II (1939-1945). Many commentators and readers have seen a parallel between Sauron and Adolf Hitler, and the Ring of Power is sometimes thought of as the atomic bomb that ended the war, like Mt. Doom exploding when the Ring was thrown in. Tolkien has repeatedly denied the intention of such allegory. In the Foreword to the second edition, he states that his story is not an allegory, but has "applicability." A mythic story is universal and should be relevant to any time, for the same principles apply, age after age.

Nevertheless, Tolkien's experience in the trenches of World War I, where many of his friends were killed, and his son Christopher's experience in World War II certainly weave in the flavor and concerns of the first half of the twentieth century. Tom Shippey credits Tolkien with being a twentieth-century author depicting evil in a new, impersonal way that fits the angst of his generation. He calls it "the wraithing-process" where one becomes gradually emptied of a moral responsibility. In a modern age, no one seems personally responsible for evil; it is decentralized and administered by wraith-like people who have lost their will (e.g., the Ringwraiths).

Critique of Modernism

Tolkien's myth, though not set in the contemporary world, is clearly a critique of modernism, and perhaps the best way he knew to stage such a critique was to set the story in ancient times. Modernism, from Tolkien's perspective, is not just free form in literature, but a way of thinking, cut loose from traditional roots and values. His disgust with the pollution caused by industrialism, for instance, which values money over the environment, vents itself in the episode of Saruman's cutting down trees for his war furnaces. It has been said that the tremendous popularity of *The Lord of the Rings* is due to its reference to an older, more traditional world where humans have clear relationship both to the spiritual and natural worlds, thus satisfying generations of readers who long for an alternative vision of life.

The Inklings

Tolkien and his friends, C. S. Lewis and Charles Williams, were part of a group of Oxford dons who met together in the 1930s and 1940s to read their writing aloud to one another. Their club was called The Inklings, and many fantasy books came out it, such as *The Lord of the Rings* and the Narnia books. These men were generally opposed to modernist writers and thinkers, having more religious, philological, philosophical, and theological interests. Tolkien was a devout Catholic, and though he did not write specifically about his religion, it informs his myth and values.

Critical Overview

When *The Lord of the Rings* was published in three parts, one at a time during 1954 and 1955 (*The Fellowship of the Ring, The Two Towers,* and *The Return of the King*) it garnered a mixed reception. Reviewers loved it or hated it. It was not taken seriously by the literary establishment, for there was nothing comparable in modern fiction: the work was the first modern adult fantasy novel. Edmund Wilson was one of those intellectuals who found it repulsive, and as quoted in *The Tolkien Scrapbook* in his article for *Nation* in 1956, Wilson calls it "juvenile trash," a fantasy for its own sake. He claims it is written by an amateur who does not understand literary form and that the hero undergoes no real temptations. One can feel Wilson wanting to quickly stamp out the enthusiasm of the few before it is fanned into a flame.

W. H. Auden, the well-known English poet (also quoted in *The Tolkien Scrapbook* and in the same year in the *New York Times Book Review*), supported Tolkien's work, calling the book "a masterpiece of its genre" and describing it as a heroic quest. He further asserts Tolkien succeeds, as Milton does not, in representing the good as a fuller, more imaginative reality than evil. Comparison of *The Lord of the Rings* by admirers to great epic literature irked scholars such as Wilson.

Tolkien's friend and fellow Inkling, C. S.

Lewis, defended the work. In "Tolkien's *The Lord of the Rings*," Lewis calls it "lightning from a clear sky," and he argues that it should be taken seriously as a moral depiction of good and evil, that the book is full of the experience of his generation who lived through World War I. He asserts that myth is a valuable tool for understanding the world.

Neil Isaacs, in his essay "On the Possibility of Writing Tolkien Criticism" in *Tolkien and His Critics*, points out that the popularity of the book gets in the way of its being taken seriously as literature. He refers to the fact that in the 1960s Ace Publishing came out with an illegal paperback version, and *The Lord of the Rings* became an overnight cult favorite on American college campuses. Some critics felt that an adolescent craze cannot be literature and assumed interest would die out.

Fifty years after its first appearance, *The Lord of the Rings* was widely viewed as serious literature. The work serves as the foundation of the popular fantasy industry and prompted whole areas of critical investigation, such as Tolkien Studies and Middle-Earth Studies. It appealed to something vital in so many people that T. A. Shippey, in his 2001 study *J. R. R. Tolkien: Author of the Century*, claimed Tolkien as the most important author of the twentieth century, over such giants as James Joyce.

Sources

Anderson, Poul, "Awakening the Elves," in *Meditations on Middle-Earth*, St. Martin's Griffin, 2001, p. 26.

Auden, W. H., "At the End of the Quest, Victory," in *A Tolkien Scrapbook*, edited by Alida Becker, Running Press, 1978, p. 44; originally published in *New York Times Book Review*, January 22, 1956.

Campbell, Joseph, *The Hero with a Thousand Faces*, Princeton University Press, 1949, pp. 4, 39.

Card, Orson Scott, "How Tolkien Means," in *Meditations on Middle-Earth*, St. Martin's Griffin, 2001, p. 160.

Carpenter, Humphrey, *J. R. R. Tolkien: A Biography*, Houghton Mifflin, 2000, p.138.

Isaacs, Neil D., "On the Possibility of Writing Tolkien Criticism," in *Tolkien and the Critics: Essays on J. R. R. Tolkien's "The Lord of the Rings,"* edited by Neil D. Isaacs and Rose A. Zimbardo, University of Notre Dame Press, 1968.

Le Guin, Ursula K., "Rhythmic Pattern in *The Lord of the Rings*," in *Meditations on Middle-Earth*, St. Martin's Griffin, 2001, pp. 102, 103.

Lewis, C. S., "Tolkien's *The Lord of the Rings*," in *Of This and Other Worlds*, edited by Walter Hooper, Collins, 1982, p.112.

Manlove, C. N., "J. R. R. Tolkien (1892-1973) and

The Lord of the Rings," in *Modern Fantasy: Five Studies*, Cambridge University Press, 1975, p. 194.

Pratchett, Terry, "Cult Classic," in *Meditations on Middle-Earth*, St. Martin's Griffin, 2001, p. 80.

Shippey, T. A., *J. R. R. Tolkien: Author of the Century*, Houghton Mifflin, 2000, p. 125.

Tolkien, J. R. R., *The Lord of the Rings*, Houghton Mifflin, 1994.

————, "On Fairy-Stories," in *The Monsters and the Critics and Other Essays*, edited by Christopher Tolkien, George Allen & Unwin, 1983, pp. 109, 116, 132, 138, 143.

Wilson, Edmund, "Oo, Those Awful Orcs," in *A Tolkien Scrapbook*, edited by Alida Becker, Running Press, 1978, p. 55; originally published in *Nation*, April 14, 1956.

Further Reading

Carpenter, Humphrey, *The Inklings: C. S. Lewis, J. R. R. Tolkien, Charles Williams, and their Friends*, Houghton Mifflin, 1979.

> Carpenter interweaves biographical background about the three friends with actual reconstructions of meetings of the Inklings, a club of Oxford professors and writers who read their work aloud to one another. In this circle, Tolkien tested drafts of *The Lord of the Rings.*

————, *J. R. R. Tolkien: A Biography*, Houghton Mifflin, 1987.

> Carpenter is able to take the seemingly boring life of a professor and illuminate it as the rich leaf mold of an artist's inner world. He integrates the main events of Tolkien's life with the themes and content of his books. This is the official biography; Carpenter was given unrestricted access to papers and interviewed friends and family. It is very entertaining, a glimpse into both the internal and external life of an Oxford don.

Carpenter, Humphrey, and Christopher Tolkien, *The*

Letters of J. R. R. Tolkien, Houghton Mifflin, 2000.

> The letters of Tolkien illuminate like no commentator can the richness of the novel. This collection is like another appendix based on readers' questions with many details of the story further developed. His letters explain his background myths and the characters' fates in the novel.

Haber, Karen, ed., *Meditations on Middle-Earth*, St. Martin's Griffin, 2001.

> In this anthology, major science fiction and fantasy writers, such as Ursula Le Guin, Raymond Feist, Poul Anderson, Terry Pratchett, George R. R. Martin, and many others, tell how they discovered Tolkien and how he inspired their desire to write. The book is informative in many directions at once, giving deep insights into Tolkien's work and its legacy, as well as into the creative process of writing fantasy. The book was nominated for the 2002 Hugo and Locus awards.

Hammond, Wayne G., and Christina Scull, *J. R. R. Tolkien: Artist and Illustrator*, Houghton Mifflin, 1995.

> Tolkien is recognized as an illustrator as well as a writer, and

though his own drawings appear in books and calendars, many have never been published before this publication. This fascinating book shows the range of his subjects and how he used drawings and maps to think out his stories. Such details as coats of arms and Numenorean fabric design are included.

Perkins, Agnes, and Helen Hill, "The Corruption of Power," in *A Tolkien Compass*, edited by Jared Lobdell, Open Court, 2003, pp. 55-65.

This article discusses how even the desire for power corrupts the characters in *The Lord of the Rings.* The authors conclude that the theme is timely because the demand for power in contemporary politics continues to increase from all sides, and the dangers need to be spelled out. The other articles in this anthology are equally helpful.

CPSIA information can be obtained
at www.ICGtesting.com
Printed in the USA
BVHW031455300822
645844BV00010B/502